TUNNELS

A TRUE BOOK

by
Elaine Landau

Children's Press®
A Division of Scholastic Inc.

New York Toronto London Auckland Sydney
Mexico City New Delhi Hong Kong
Danbury, Connecticut

A family rides their bikes out of an old railroad tunnel.

Author's Dedication:
To Joshua Garmizo

Visit Children's Press® on the
Internet at:
http://publishing.grolier.com

Library of Congress Cataloging-in-Publication Data

Landau, Elaine.
    Tunnels / by Elaine Landau
        p. cm. — (A true book)
    Includes bibliographical references and index.
    ISBN 0-516-22185-X (lib. bdg.)   ISBN 0-516-27325-6 (pbk.)
    1. Tunnels—Juvenile literature. 2. Tunneling—Juvenile literature.
[1. Tunnels. 2. Tunneling.] I. Title. II. Series.
TA807 .L36 2001
624.1'9—dc21   00-030700

Contents

Subways use tunnels to help people travel around a city.

Underground Passages

People have built tunnels since early times. The ancient Romans used tunnels to help them win battles. Their enemies built walls around their cities for protection, but that did not stop the Romans. Roman soldiers dug tunnels under the walls to get inside the cities and attack. These attacks took their enemies by surprise.

Today, tunnels help us get where we want to go. They provide faster, safer routes through mountains and beneath cities. Cars and trains use underwater tunnels to cross rivers and other bodies of water. People travel around cities in subways—networks of underground tunnels. All these vital passageways shorten our journeys.

Millions of people travel through tunnels every day.

Building Tunnels

Building a tunnel is always hard work. First, engineers study the land where the tunnel is going to be built. Constructing a tunnel that runs through a mountain requires different methods and machinery than building one underwater.

These workers are building a railroad tunnel in Pennsylvania.

Builders use explosives to make tunnels through rock.

To build a tunnel through rock, blasting is usually necessary. Workers drill holes in the rock and fill them with explosives. The explosives are then set off. After the explosion, the broken pieces of rock are carried out. The broken pieces are called muck. Sometimes workers will spray a rock tunnel with concrete to prevent broken pieces of rock from falling into it.

When a tunnel is dug out of limestone, slate, or gravel, blasting may not be necessary. Here workers use tunnel-boring

machines instead. Disk cutters attached to these machines chop away at the rock.

Digging a tunnel through clay, sand, or a muddy riverbed may seem easier, but it is more dangerous. These soft substances can cause cave-ins. Usually, when a tunnel is dug through these materials, the workers are protected by an airtight cylinder called a shield. The shield is slowly pushed through the earth while the workers install a lining of concrete or cast iron in the

This machine keeps workers safe while building a tunnel.

TML   EURO TUNNEL

tunnel. As the shield moves forward, the work proceeds section by section.

Going Underwater

When you think of a tunnel, you may picture a passage through earth or rock. However, some tunnels are across the bottom of a body of water. These are called submerged tunnels. Submerged tunnels are sometimes needed to link land areas that could otherwise be reached only by boat.

These people are working on underwater tunnels.

Often these tunnels are constructed by the "cut and cover" method. First a trench is dug across the bottom of a waterway. Steel or concrete tunnel sections are then floated over the trench and are dropped into place. Divers fasten the sections together. Usually these underwater tunnels are covered over with soil.

Engineers plan carefully before building a tunnel. They study the surrounding land to determine what kind of tunnel will be best. They decide where to build the tunnel and they figure out how much it will cost.

The Holland Tunnel

Thousands of cars, trucks, and buses drive through the Holland Tunnel every day. This tunnel connects New York City with New Jersey via the Hudson River. By the time its construction began in 1920, the tunnel was badly needed. The only way vehicles could

A crowd gathers for the opening of the Holland Tunnel.

come into New York City from New Jersey was by ferryboat. And with 24,000 New Jersey vehicles entering and leaving New York City every day— that system was strained.

The Holland Tunnel is 1.5 miles (2 km) long. It consists of two huge tubes through which the vehicles travel. All motor-traffic tunnels have a problem with the exhaust fumes given off by vehicles. In shorter tunnels, the problem

A truck and a bus drive
through the Holland Tunnel.

is usually solved by having air flow in one end of the tunnel and out the other. However, in a passageway as long as the Holland Tunnel, that system would not work.

The project's engineer, Clifford M. Holland, came up with the answer. He created an airflow system with two air ducts—one air duct running beneath each tube's roadway and another air duct running above it. Forty-two

Clifford M. Holland

giant fans drew air into the
lower duct and sent it out to
the roadway through slots. A

second set of fans pulled exhaust fumes into the upper duct. These were sent out of the tubes through slots in the ceiling.

Holland spent nearly all his time at the construction site. Unfortunately, he did not live to see his master-piece. He died of a heart attack three years before its completion. However, the tunnel still bears his name.

The St. Gotthard Tunnels

The St. Gotthard tunnels run through the central Alps and connect Switzerland with northern Italy. There are two St. Gotthard tunnels. The first to be built was a 9-mile (14-km) railroad tunnel. It was constructed over a century ago between 1872 and 1882.

An early photograph of the St. Gotthard train tunnel

Completing this mountain tunnel was very dangerous and difficult. There were drilling and flooding problems. During its construction, 310 workers were killed and 877 others were injured.

The second tunnel is for automobiles and runs parallel to the railroad tunnel. Known as the St. Gotthard Road Tunnel, it is the world's longest highway tunnel at about 10 miles (16 km) long.

The St. Gotthard tunnels today

Completed in 1980, the St. Gotthard Road Tunnel was not as hard to build as the railway tunnel. However, the workers had some problems with flooding and it took them five months to dig through the rubble from the rail tunnel. All that hard work has paid off—this tunnel through the Swiss Alps connected many parts of Europe. Today, a driver can go from Hamburg, Germany, to southern Italy without ever leaving the road!

The Chunnel

The Channel Tunnel forms a railway link between the countries of Britain and France. The Channel Tunnel, or "Chunnel," was built beneath the waters of the English Channel. It opened to the public in 1994.

Workers build the Chunnel in Britain (left) and in France (below).

A family drives their car onto a train (above) that takes them into the Chunnel (opposite).

The Chunnel meets a number of important transportation needs. High-speed passenger trains and vehicle-carrying shuttle trains use the tunnel.

Freight trains also rely on the Chunnel.

The Channel Tunnel stretches 31 miles (50 km) from Folkstone, England, to Conquelles, France.

It is made up of three large tubes. Two are used for railway traffic. The third tube provides the other two with fresh air and can serve as an emergency exit, if needed, and as an entrance and exit for maintenance crews. All three tubes are connected at several points by specially designed passages.

To complete the Channel Tunnel, engineers had many problems to overcome.

Workers from Britain and France shake hands.

Since the tunnel connected Britain and France, the builders had to please two governments, work in two languages, and follow two sets of safety and legal codes.

The tunnel cost $12 billion to build, but the end result was well worth the cost and the effort. People from around the world now use the tunnel.

Underground Railways

Subways are underground railways. They are made up of a large and complex network of tunnels. Subways are designed to take people quickly where they want to go. These transportation systems are common in large cities where heavy traffic

A subway in
Los Angeles,
California

often makes traveling by car
or bus difficult and slow.
The world's first subway
system began operating in

1863 in London, England. In time, many large American cities built subways too.

An entrance to London's subway system called the Underground

Passengers wait to get on Chicago's new subway in 1943.

These underground systems provided a speedy and low-cost way of getting around. By 1897, Boston's subway system had opened. Now, Atlanta, Baltimore, Chicago, New York, Philadelphia, San Francisco, and Washington, D.C., all have subways.

Today, New York City has the world's largest subway system and has added a special feature—dual lines. This allows express trains to travel rapidly on a separate track while local trains on another track make all stops along a route. The express service allows passengers to save time.

When people think of large cities, they often think of towering skyscrapers. But in many places, tunnels allow these cities to also operate underground.

People crowd into subway cars in New York City.

To Find Out More

Here are some additional resources to help you learn more about tunnels:

 **Books**

Darling, David J. **Could You Ever Dig A Hole To China?** Dillon Press, 1990.

Dunn, Andrew. **Tunnels.** Thomson Learning, 1993.

Gaff, Jackie. **Buildings, Bridges, & Tunnels.** Random House, 1991.

Hunter, Ryan Ann. **Dig a Tunnel.** Holiday House, 1992.

Richardson, Joy. **Tunnels.** Franklin Watts, 1994.

Royston, Angela. **Buildings, Bridges and Tunnels.** Warwick Press, 1991.

Sauvain, Philip Arthur. **Tunnels.** Garrett Educational Corp., 1990.

Spangenburg, Ray. **The Story of America's Tunnels.** Facts On File, 1993.

Yepsen, Roger, B. **City Trains: Moving Through America's Cities by Rail.** Macmillan Publishing Co., 1993.

Organizations and Online Sites

New York City Subway System

http://www.nycsubway.org

Learn about the history and everyday operation of the world's largest subway system.

Chicago Tunnel Company Railroad

http://www.ameritech.net/ users/chicagotunnel/ tunnel1.html

A web site dedicated to preserving the history of Chicago's unique little rail-road. Read about the 60-mile (96 km) electric rail-road that once operated in small tunnels 40 feet (12 m) below the streets of down-town Chicago.

Buildings, Bridges, and Tunnels

http://www.discovery.com/

This online site, a compan-ion to a Discovery Channel documentary, offers images, information, and a timeline on tunnels.

Important Words

blasting shattering by explosives

dual lines separate tracks in a rail system for express and local trains

duct a tube or passage that carries a substance, such as air

muck the broken pieces of rock that result from blasting a tunnel

riverbed the bed or channel a river flows through

rubble rough, irregular pieces of rock

shield an airtight steel cylinder used to protect workers digging a tunnel through clay, sand, or other soft substances

submerged tunnel a tunnel built underwater

subway a system of underground railways

Index

Meet the Author

Award-winning author Elaine Landau worked as a newspaper reporter, an editor, and a youth services librarian before becoming a full-time writer. She has written more than one hundred and fifty nonfiction books for young people, including True Books on dinosaurs, animals, countries, and food.

Ms. Landau, who has a bachelor's degree in English and journalism from New York University and a master's degree in library and information science from Pratt Institute, lives in Florida with her husband and son.